I0436643

Trump

The man who would be bling

Picture of a fence in Asbury Park, NJ

Poems by John Haigis
(610) 809-4856
JHDarby@gmail.com

Contents

A Bully with Bling and with Bluster

A bully with bling and with bluster
The persona projected by Trump
A whole heaping plate of crap custard
And maybe a bit of mugwump

His fans see him as an outsider
His lack of experience a plus
Conspicuous lack of credentials
Plainspoken, though often a cuss

I don't know what it could mean for the country
If Commander-in-Chief he becomes
I fear for more hatred and carnage
And well-being in negative sums

The Candidate

He may not be an evil man
He might even love the nation
But listening to his rants on stage
Brings angst and consternation

He uses demagoguery
And puts all others down
And yet he thinks that he's the one
To wear the golden crown

The one who would be President
Must have a level head
The stakes are high lest you and I
End up so very dead

Are We Ready?

A racist misogynist with a hair trigger
Not the most statesman-like public figure
Somehow he has been selected
And possibly could be elected
To be our leader strong and steady
Good Lord, I hope we all are ready
To let all our bad angels out
And knock some immigrants about
Because it's somehow more than an even bet
That what we've seen, is what we'll get!

Annabel Trump
(Apologies to Edgar Allen Poe)

It was not so very long ago
In a kingdom by the sea
That a bright orange man
Thought that he should be King
And would get there
By bluster and bling

He was like a big child
And not very mild
In his kingdom by the sea
And his outrageous quotes
Would garner him votes
Most disturbing to hear and to see

He wanted a wall so high and so tall
To keep all the Mexicans out
It did not seem to matter
That they've been here for years
He did not have a quibble or doubt

Annabel Trump (continued)

All new Muslims he'd ban
Or at least that's the plan
Regardless of faith or the facts
Painting all in a rush
With a very broad brush
In the light of Orlando attacks

Never mind he was wrong
The perp here all along
Native born but his parents were foreign
Just like millions of others
And their sisters and brothers
Immigration for years has been soarin'

But the facts do not matter
In delusional chatter
And a quest to make America great
To learn what's going on
One must think hard and long
And that's something even he cannot fake

Alice in Wonderland

Globalization

He decries the situation
We've all helped to create
That everything we see or buy
Is not made in the States

We buy because it's cheaper
We do not want to pay
The somewhat higher prices
For "made in the USA"

Clothing, tools and cameras
We buy from overseas
We're buying the convenience
Sometimes we buy the sleaze

With sweatshop exploitation
For the sake of lower wages
We do not count the human cost
Or economic cages

For the workers it's a bonus
Just to have a job
And a way to help their families
Amidst the hungry mob

In any global village though
You'll find a share of poor
Perhaps if we keep them over there
They'll not be at our door?

He Who Has Been Named Too Much

He who has been named too much
Has entered into our brains
Reflecting deep division
And fomenting the same

I would like to treat him as a joke
But he really isn't humorous
The side show that we've all endured
Is somewhat toxic-tumorous

A candidate with quite thin skin
Sings praises to mass killers
And thinks he should be President
One of our nation's pillars

A siren song of prejudice,
Ignorance, and hate,
Is not the way, in my small view
To make our country great

But there it is, as what will be
Who knows what we'll become?
What landscape for our progeny
When all this mess is done?

Trumpy

He's rich but a long way from classy
He says America once more will be great
When we kick out all people of color
And show them the wall or the gate

But still come this January
He may raise his hand in an oath
And somehow govern our nation
An outcome for which I am loath

Gunga Dim
(With Apologies to Rudyard Kipling)

We may want to drown in beer, or at least to shed a tear,
When we ponder on the state of our elections
For the outcome isn't clear, and there's not so much to cheer
In the matter of a running mate selection

Some time ago Ted Cruz, decided then to choose
Carly Fiorina as his running mate
So in thinking of that choice, of another strident voice
It may give our Trump a cause to contemplate

For it's Trump, Trump, Trump
Who the primaries gave a bump
On his way to the Republican convention
At some point he'll need to state
His choice of a running mate
And till he does there may be dynamic tension

But the answer may be obvious, for a cranium so osseous
On the best way he can balance off the ticket
Someone who shares his views, and who also can amuse
But the logic of his choice may make one nauseous

He can cast his nets quite wide, before he must decide
Who is the best companion on the shelf
For he now is on a mission for an anti-politician
And who could be a better choice than he himself?

It could be Trump and Trump, standing on the stump
Expounding on their multiple positions
They both can do the dance, depending on the audience
In a powerful self-loving coalition.

Orlando

In the cold and harsh light of Orlando
America is still number one
In sorrow, and killing, and hatred
And enhanced easy access to guns

We can blame it on different religions
Jihad or a hatred of gays
With a dollop of mental disturbance
In a complex media-driven haze.

At the bottom is more human carnage
Many lives changed or brought to an end
While the death toll statistics keep rising
And mass shootings make news once again

Trumpty Dumpty

(Spoken)

Trumpty Dumpty wanted a wall
Trumpty Dumpty will campaign this fall
All the king's horse parts and some of the men
Believe that can make our land great once again

(Tune: Little Red Wing)

There once was a very rich man
Who told the world he can
Make America great again
With a big high wall and a Muslim ban

He won the primaries,
With bombast, threats and sleaze
Self-serving stew is nothing new
What's surprising is the ease

Oh we won't let these bullies take our country
Trumpty Dumpty, won't take our country
We will see how people vote come this November
If they remember, the stakes are high.

AMERICAN MODEL BUILDER

Boys Wanted for the "American Army"

Good pay in lots of fun—excellent mental train-
ing—recruiting stations at stores in your town

Thousands upon thousands of boys have enlisted in this army. They camp on the Field of Fun recruited not to fight, but to **build.**

"Armed" with an American Model Builder outfit, each boy builds all the things that great engineers build—big disappearing guns, like the one shown above; warships, aeroplanes; hoist bridges; traveling cranes; stationary engines; derricks; automobiles; printing presses; elevators; and hundreds of other models that **really operate.**

Join the ranks of the American Model Builders, fellows! It's bully fun! Tell Dad tonight that you want to enlist with the "army" Christmas morning.

Tell him that the American Model Builder is—

Best Value

—because it contains 15% **more** new and novel parts than any other outfit, such as real automobile wheels, car wheels, truck frames, bolster plates, "T" strips, ratchet pawls, new gears, and angle irons.

—because you can build **more** practical working models, models that go through all the operations of the real machines. And that's half the fun, fellows—running the models after you build 'em!

Look, Fellows!

Electric Motor Included
with Sets at $2.00 and up

Not a toy, but a real motor that will operate the models you build with your American Model Builder outfit. It has three-pole armature, spring tension brushes, form wound coils, stands 3⅛" high by 2¼" over shaft, has start, stop and reverse switch. Can be operated on dry cells or on city current through our inexpensive transformer.

—because the American Model Builder is built to last. It contains not a single piece of flimsy wood, tin or iron. Every part is made of the highest-grade brass and cold-rolled steel, double-plated. And see the panel to the left!

Fathers and Mothers

Here is the toy your boy **needs.** The American Model Builder contains all the major parts used in modern engineering and is based on correct mechanical principles. It will teach your boy to think **constructively,** fostering his inventive and creative genius. It will keep him **quiet,** amused for hours.

Ask Your Dealer

to show you the new sets of the American Model Builder and the new instruction book containing dozens of new models never before built with a construction set. He will also give you a booklet showing the new features. If your dealer hasn't the genuine American Model Builder write us and we will send catalog and full information with name of dealer who can supply you.

THE AMERICAN
MECHANICAL TOY CO.

500 First Street

Dayton   -   -   -   Ohio

Get in the Big Prize Contest for new models. 155 prizes valued up to $100 each. Write us for details.

Ad from St Nicholas Magazine, 1917

David Duke Now Thinks

David Duke now thinks the Jews
Are behind Mr. Trump's opposition
In this I think he's missed the point
In his extreme position

It's true the Jews do very well
Like many other folk
Hard work and brains often succeed
Hatred is far from a joke

Throughout their history they've been oppressed
And hated just for being
They've dealt with things that came their way
A wider picture seeing

Pogroms and hatred have come their way
Remembered holocaust
Living as their God commands
At such enormous cost

The Campaign

How much is media?
How much is hype?
How much is politics?
How much is tripe?

Trump makes good copy
Leads in the news
The more he outrageously
Expresses his views

So here are some poems
Which I did write
He'll enjoy them as long as
I spell his name right

We Need to Know What's Going On

We need to know what's going on
Perhaps we never will
The news is full of carnage
And many folks who kill

We seek to find the reason
Why innocents should die
It's more than just the payback
Of an eye for the loss of an eye

Hatred feeds upon itself
The "Us" who fears the "Other"
When in fact we all are, at our core
The child of the same mother

The Earth who gave birth to us all
Created by our God
In light of this, to kill and hate
Seems to me quite odd

The Earth.

The Political Debates, 2015

Are they all delusional?
Or just playing to their base?
The candidates on full display
Standing in debate

I'll build a wall...I'll deport them all
I'll make us strong and free
After all, walls work so well
For the Israelis

Government's an evil thing
Let's get rid of regulation
The golden age as it used to be
When we were a new nation

Sweat shops, cholera, the seven-day week
Child labor and robber barons,
Ah those sure were the good old days
There is just no comparison

My folks were poor but now I'm rich
The way it ought to be
I did it all by the sweat of my brow
(And occasional subsidy?)

Take the fetters off big business
And certainly off the banks...
We'll let them fall, we'll let them fail
We'll let them all just tank

(**Political Debates**, continued)

But never regulate them
That's not our chosen way
What ever could go wrong with that?
It's not us who will pay.

We rich are doing very well
Thank you very much
We get to blame the Democrats
Or Socialists and such

No-Fly zones are needed
To show them we are tough
Who cares if we will start a war?
We all have had enough

Of appearing indecisive
By thinking these things through
We want to get elected
We know what we must do

We don't know who we're arming
But we must stand up to Putin
Let's throw more gas on the funeral pyre
How much gas we're disputing

We all are right, and firm, and sage
And qualified to lead
As God's our witness, even though
It's not us who will bleed

Exclusions

Let's keep out all the Muslims,
And everyone who disagrees
The only one left will then be.........me

We need to know what's going on?
Perhaps we never will
Especially if we act before we think
And simply kill

The old knee jerk reaction,
The jerk part is quite apt
We'll give a lesson on how to hate....
In cycles we get trapped

A king named Hammurabi
Once decreed a code
A guide for actions in his lands
The duties that were owed

An "eye for an eye" is the shorthand way
We remember this designation
But what if that was meant to be
A form of limitation?

ONLY an eye for the loss of an eye
Only a hand for a hand
Not an eye, and a hand, and a leg
Could we understand?

Our lives have friction and conflicts
We don't always agree
But seeing the other's point of view
Helps peace to thrive and be.

VACATION TIME.
The way the world seems to him since she has left.

The Battle of the Bogeyman
(After seeing the movie Bridge of Spies)

The battle of the bogeyman,
Useful to us all
Both sides use them frequently
The people to enthrall

"The Soviets want to hurt us"
"The capitalists want our doom"
"We must get them or they'll get us"
Armageddon looms.

A scarcity of resources
"As long as we get ours"
Justifying anything
Viewed from ivory towers

And in the trenches poor lost souls
Who don't want any harm;
Pawns and lives expendable
Roused by dread alarms

FINALE.

Finale? Or in the words of the Wicked Witch of the West, "Is our little party just beginning?"